KANSAS
DRIVER'S LICENSE
HANDBOOK 2024

Your Complete Guide to Safe and
Legal Driving

Jorge N. Miller

Table of Contents

CHAPTER 1: INTRODUCTION TO KANSAS DRIVING

Driving in Kansas requires a thorough understanding of the rules, responsibilities, and privileges associated with holding a driver's license. This chapter provides a comprehensive overview, covering the importance of a driver's license, the various types and classes available in Kansas, and the procedures for obtaining and renewing a driver's license.

Understanding the Importance of a Driver's License

A driver's license serves as more than just a legal document permitting individuals to operate a vehicle; it represents a significant responsibility and privilege. In Kansas, driving is regulated to ensure the safety of all road users, and a driver's license signifies that an individual has demonstrated the knowledge, skills, and competence required to operate a motor vehicle safely and responsibly.

Obtaining a driver's license is often a rite of passage, marking a transition to adulthood and independence. It grants individuals the freedom to travel independently, commute to work or school, and participate in various aspects of daily life that require personal transportation. However, with this privilege comes the responsibility to adhere to traffic laws, respect other road users, and prioritize safety at all times.

Kansas Driver's License Types and Classes

Kansas offers different types and classes of driver's licenses, each tailored to specific driving privileges and vehicle types. Understanding these classifications is essential for determining the type of license you need based on your driving needs and the vehicles you intend to operate.

1. Class A, B, C, and M Licenses: These classes categorize licenses based on the type of vehicle being operated and the weight or capacity of the vehicle.

2. Class D and G Licenses: These are typically for standard passenger vehicles and motorcycles, respectively.

3. Provisional Licenses: Kansas also offers provisional licenses for younger drivers, which come with specific restrictions and requirements until certain criteria are met.

Each class and type of license may have different testing requirements and restrictions. It's crucial to choose the correct license type that aligns with your driving intentions to ensure legal compliance and safety on the road.

Obtaining and Renewing a Driver's License

The process of obtaining a driver's license in Kansas involves several steps designed to assess an individual's knowledge of traffic laws, understanding of safe driving practices, and ability to operate a vehicle competently. Key steps include:

- Applying for a License: Applicants must meet minimum age requirements and provide necessary identification documents, such as proof of identity, residency, and Social Security number.

- Knowledge Testing: Applicants are required to pass a written knowledge test covering traffic laws, road signs, and safe driving practices.

- Road Skills Testing: Upon passing the knowledge test, applicants must demonstrate their ability to operate a vehicle safely during a road skills test conducted by a licensed examiner.

- Vision Screening and Medical Requirements: Applicants must meet minimum vision standards and may be required to provide medical certification in certain circumstances.

Renewing a driver's license in Kansas is necessary to maintain legal driving privileges. Licenses typically expire after a set period, and renewal procedures vary depending on the driver's age and license class. Renewal requirements often include passing a vision screening and paying a renewal fee. Kansas also offers online renewal options for eligible drivers, streamlining the process for those who qualify.

Understanding the process of obtaining and renewing a driver's license ensures compliance with Kansas state laws and regulations, contributing to safer roadways and promoting responsible driving practices among residents. By familiarizing oneself with these requirements and responsibilities, individuals can confidently navigate the process of acquiring and maintaining a Kansas driver's license while prioritizing safety and legal compliance on the road.

Exam questions

1. Question: What is the primary purpose of a driver's license in Kansas?

A) Proof of residency

B) Permission to operate a motor vehicle

C) Identification for voting

D) Access to public transportation

Correct Answer: B) Permission to operate a motor vehicle

2. Question: Which of the following does a driver's license signify in Kansas?

A) Ability to travel internationally

B) Competence in vehicle maintenance

C) Legal authority to operate a vehicle

D) Access to discounted vehicle insurance rates

Correct Answer: C) Legal authority to operate a vehicle

3. Question: What are the main types of driver's licenses available in Kansas?

A) Class A, B, C, D, G, and M

B) Class X, Y, Z, and W

C) Class 1, 2, 3, and 4

D) Class P, Q, R, and S

Correct Answer: A) Class A, B, C, D, G, and M

4. Question: What type of license is required for operating motorcycles in Kansas?

   A) Class G

   B) Class C

   C) Class M

   D) Class D

   Correct Answer: C) Class M

5. Question: Which license class is typically required for operating commercial vehicles in Kansas?

   A) Class D

   B) Class C

   C) Class M

   D) Class A

   Correct Answer: D) Class A

6. Question: What is a provisional driver's license in Kansas?

A) A license for temporary visitors

B) A license for drivers under 21 years old

C) A license for seniors over 65 years old

D) A license for individuals with medical conditions

Correct Answer: B) A license for drivers under 21 years old

7. Question: How often must a driver's license be renewed in Kansas?

A) Every 2 years

B) Every 5 years

C) Every 8 years

D) Every 10 years

Correct Answer: C) Every 8 years

8. Question: What is required to renew a driver's license in Kansas?

A) Passing a physical fitness test

B) Passing a written knowledge test

C) Passing a vision screening

D) Passing a road skills test

Correct Answer: C) Passing a vision screening

9. Question: What is the first step in applying for a driver's license in Kansas?

A) Paying a licensing fee

B) Passing a written knowledge test

C) Providing proof of identity and residency

D) Completing a driver education course

Correct Answer: C) Providing proof of identity and residency

10. Question: Who administers the road skills test for obtaining a driver's license in Kansas?

A) Local police department

B) Kansas Department of Transportation (KDOT)

C) Licensed driving instructor

D) Certified examiner at a driver's license office

Correct Answer: D) Certified examiner at a driver's license office

CHAPTER 2: TRAFFIC LAWS AND REGULATIONS

Understanding traffic laws and regulations is crucial for safe and legal driving in Kansas. This chapter covers various aspects including traffic signs, signals, road markings, right-of-way rules, responsibilities, speed limits, and safe speeding practices.

TRAFFIC LIGHT (STOP / WATCH CAREFULLY / GO AHEAD)		ONE WAY	STOP HERE	SPEED LIMIT	CONSTRUCTION ZONE
RAILWAY CROSSING (Guarded)	RAILWAY CROSSING (Unguarded)	ZEBRA CROSSING	SCHOOL AHEAD	BUS ZONE	CYCLE ZONE
NARROW ROAD (Left) AHEAD	NARROW ROAD AHEAD	NARROW ROAD (Right) AHEAD	TWO-WAY TRAFFIC	AIRPORT AHEAD	ANIMAL ZONE
RIGHT ZIGZAG BEND	LEFT ZIGZAG BEND	RIGHT CURVE	LEFT CURVE	BUMPS	SPEED-BREAKER
ROAD CLOSED	PARKING	NO PARKING	NO AUTOMOBILES	NO TRUCKS	NO HORN
MEN AT WORK	LEFT TURN	CROSSROADS	RIGHT TURN	ROUGH ROAD AHEAD	LANDSLIDE AHEAD
HOSPITAL AHEAD	NO LEFT TURN	NO ENTRY	NO RIGHT TURN	DRIVE SAFELY	ACCIDENT-PRONE AREA
END OF SPEED LIMIT	OVERTAKING PROHIBITED	STEEP HILL	NARROW BRIDGE	U-TURN	NO U-TURN

21

Traffic Signs, Signals, and Road Markings

Traffic signs, signals, and road markings provide essential information and guidance to drivers, ensuring safe navigation on roads. In Kansas, these visual cues are categorized into three main types:

1. Regulatory Signs: These signs inform drivers of laws and regulations that must be obeyed, such as speed limits, no parking zones, and lane usage.

2. Warning Signs: Warning signs alert drivers to potential hazards ahead, such as sharp curves, pedestrian crossings, and intersections.

3. Guide Signs: Guide signs provide directional and distance information, guiding drivers to destinations, services, and highway exits.

Understanding and obeying these signs is crucial for safe driving practices and compliance with traffic laws. Drivers must be able to recognize and respond appropriately to each type of sign to prevent accidents and ensure smooth traffic flow.

Right-of-Way Rules and Responsibilities

Right-of-way rules dictate which vehicle has the legal right to proceed first in specific situations, ensuring orderly and safe traffic movement. Key right-of-way rules in Kansas include:

- Yielding to vehicles already in intersections.
- Yielding to pedestrians in crosswalks.
- Yielding to emergency vehicles with sirens and lights activated.
- Obeying traffic signals and signs that govern right-of-way.

Understanding and respecting right-of-way rules is essential to prevent collisions and maintain traffic efficiency. Violating right-of-way laws can result in accidents, fines, and legal consequences.

Speed Limits and Safe Speeding Practices

Speed limits in Kansas are established to promote safety and reduce the risk of accidents on roadways. Factors influencing speed limit decisions include road conditions, traffic density, and surrounding environment. Common speed limits in Kansas include:

- Residential areas typically have lower speed limits to protect pedestrians and children.
- Highways and freeways have higher speed limits to accommodate faster traffic flow.

Safe speeding practices involve:

- Adhering to posted speed limits and adjusting speed according to road and weather conditions.
- Maintaining a safe following distance from other vehicles.
- Avoiding distractions such as texting or adjusting electronics while driving.
- Using headlights appropriately in low visibility conditions.

Exceeding speed limits or driving too fast for conditions can lead to accidents, injuries, and legal penalties. Practicing safe speeding habits promotes responsible driving and enhances road safety for all users.

By understanding and adhering to traffic laws related to signs, signals, road markings, right-of-way rules, responsibilities, speed limits, and safe speeding practices, drivers in Kansas can contribute to safer roadways and a more efficient transportation system. Continual awareness and compliance with these regulations are essential for maintaining personal safety and the well-being of others on the road.

Exam questions

1. Question: What do regulatory signs indicate to drivers in Kansas?

A) Potential hazards ahead

B) Recommended driving speeds

C) Laws and regulations to follow

D) Directions to nearby services

Correct Answer: C) Laws and regulations to follow

2. Question: Which type of traffic sign warns drivers of upcoming sharp turns or intersections?

A) Regulatory signs

B) Warning signs

C) Guide signs

D) Informational signs

Correct Answer: B) Warning signs

3. Question: What is the purpose of guide signs on Kansas roadways?

A) To enforce speed limits

B) To provide directions and distances

C) To warn of potential hazards

D) To indicate laws and regulations

Correct Answer: B) To provide directions and distances

4. Question: According to Kansas traffic laws, who has the right-of-way at an uncontrolled intersection?

A) The vehicle on the right

B) The vehicle making a left turn

C) The vehicle entering from a side street

D) The vehicle traveling straight through

Correct Answer: A) The vehicle on the right

5. Question: When approaching a pedestrian crossing in Kansas, what must drivers do?

A) Continue at the same speed

B) Yield the right-of-way to pedestrians

C) Speed up to clear the crossing quickly

D) Sound the horn to alert pedestrians

Correct Answer: B) Yield the right-of-way to pedestrians

6. Question: What is the maximum speed limit in a Kansas residential area, unless otherwise posted?

A) 30 mph

B) 35 mph

C) 40 mph

D) 45 mph

Correct Answer: A) 30 mph

7. Question: In adverse weather conditions in Kansas, what should drivers do regarding their speed?

A) Maintain the posted speed limit

B) Reduce speed and increase following distance

C) Increase speed to clear the weather quickly

D) Rely on hazard lights to warn other drivers

Correct Answer: B) Reduce speed and increase following distance

8. Question: What is the legal consequence of exceeding the posted speed limit in Kansas?

A) Verbal warning by law enforcement

B) Fine and possible points on driving record

C) Automatic license suspension

D) Community service requirement

Correct Answer: B) Fine and possible points on driving record

9. Question: How should drivers interpret a yellow traffic signal in Kansas?

A) Speed up to clear the intersection

B) Stop immediately

C) Slow down and prepare to stop

D) Proceed with caution

Correct Answer: C) Slow down and prepare to stop

10. Question: When must headlights be used in Kansas?

   A) Only during nighttime hours
   B) During inclement weather conditions
   C) Both A and B
   D) Neither A nor B

Correct Answer: C) Both A and B

CHAPTER 3: RULES OF THE ROAD

Understanding the rules of the road is fundamental for safe and efficient driving in Kansas. This chapter explores important aspects such as lane usage and changing, turning, passing, merging techniques, and how to handle intersections, roundabouts, and railroad crossings effectively.

Lane Usage and Changing Lanes

Proper lane usage ensures smooth traffic flow and reduces the risk of accidents. In Kansas, drivers should adhere to the following guidelines:

- Staying in Designated Lanes: Drivers must stay within marked lanes and avoid straddling lanes or driving on the shoulder except when allowed.

- Changing Lanes Safely: Before changing lanes, drivers should use their mirrors and signal their intention to change lanes. They should check blind spots by briefly turning their heads to ensure no vehicles are in the way.

- Turning from the Correct Lane: When turning, drivers should use the appropriate lanc designated for their intended direction of travel, following road signs and markings.

Understanding and adhering to these guidelines helps maintain orderly traffic and prevents collisions caused by sudden lane changes or improper positioning on the roadway.

Turning, Passing, and Merging Techniques

Turning, passing, and merging are critical maneuvers that require careful execution to ensure safety:

- Turning: Drivers should use turn signals in advance, reduce speed, and yield to pedestrians and other vehicles with the right-of-way. Completing turns smoothly and staying within marked lanes is essential.

- Passing: Drivers should only pass when it is safe and legal to do so. They should use their turn signals, check blind spots, and ensure they have enough clear distance to safely return to their lane after passing.

- Merging: When entering a highway or merging into traffic, drivers should adjust their speed to match the flow of traffic, use turn signals to indicate their intention, and yield to vehicles already on the roadway.

These techniques promote safe interaction between vehicles and minimize the risk of accidents caused by abrupt maneuvers or failure to yield.

Handling Intersections, Roundabouts, and Railroad Crossings

Intersections, roundabouts, and railroad crossings require specific attention and adherence to traffic laws:

- Intersections: Drivers approaching intersections must obey traffic signals or signs, yield to vehicles already in the intersection, and yield to pedestrians in crosswalks.

- Roundabouts: When entering a roundabout, drivers should yield to circulating traffic, use turn signals to indicate their exit, and avoid stopping or changing lanes within the roundabout unless necessary.

- Railroad Crossings: Drivers must approach railroad crossings cautiously, obeying warning signals, stopping if necessary, and ensuring there are no trains approaching before proceeding.

Understanding and following these rules when navigating intersections, roundabouts, and railroad crossings is essential for preventing collisions and ensuring the safety of all road users.

By mastering lane usage and changing, turning, passing, merging techniques, and understanding how to handle intersections, roundabouts, and railroad crossings, drivers in Kansas can contribute to safer roadways and a more efficient transportation system. Continual practice and adherence to these rules are crucial for maintaining personal safety and the well-being of others on the road.

Exam questions

1. Question: What should drivers do before changing lanes in Kansas?

A) Use their mirrors and signal their intention

B) Honk their horn to alert other drivers

C) Come to a complete stop

D) Increase their speed

Correct Answer: A) Use their mirrors and signal their intention

2. Question: When should drivers use turn signals in Kansas?

A) Only when turning left

B) Only when turning right

C) When changing lanes or turning

D) Only when other vehicles are nearby

Correct Answer: C) When changing lanes or turning

3. Question: What is a common cause of accidents when merging onto highways in Kansas?

A) Using turn signals too early

B) Failing to yield to oncoming traffic

C) Driving too slowly

D) Not checking blind spots

Correct Answer: D) Not checking blind spots

4. Question: How should drivers handle roundabouts in Kansas?

A) Stop inside the roundabout to check for traffic

B) Yield to vehicles already in the roundabout

C) Speed up to exit quickly

D) Change lanes frequently within the roundabout

Correct Answer: B) Yield to vehicles already in the roundabout

5. Question: What is the primary rule for passing other vehicles on two-lane roads in Kansas?

A) Pass on the left, when safe and legal to do so

B) Pass on the right, when safe and legal to do so

C) Pass in the middle of the road

D) Pass only during daylight hours

Correct Answer: A) Pass on the left, when safe and legal to do so

6. Question: How should drivers approach a railroad crossing in Kansas?

A) Speed up to clear the tracks quickly

B) Stop within 5 feet of the tracks

C) Proceed cautiously, obeying warning signals

D) Change lanes before crossing the tracks

Correct Answer: C) Proceed cautiously, obeying warning signals

7. Question: What must drivers do at a flashing red traffic signal in Kansas?

A) Come to a complete stop, then proceed with caution

B) Slow down and proceed without stopping

C) Treat it like a yield sign

D) Speed up to clear the intersection quickly

Correct Answer: A) Come to a complete stop, then proceed with caution

8. Question: When are drivers required to yield the right-of-way to pedestrians in crosswalks in Kansas?

A) Only during daylight hours

B) Always, regardless of the time of day

C) Only when traffic is light

D) Only when pedestrians signal to cross

Correct Answer: B) Always, regardless of the time of day

9. Question: What does a solid white line on the right side of a roadway indicate to drivers in Kansas?

A) No passing zone

B) Passing allowed with caution

C) Speed limit zone

D) Right turn only lane

Correct Answer: A) No passing zone

10. Question: What should drivers do when approaching a yield sign in Kansas?

A) Come to a complete stop

B) Maintain current speed and ignore the sign

C) Slow down and be prepared to stop if necessary

D) Speed up to merge with traffic Correct Answer: C) Slow down and be prepared to stop if necessary

CHAPTER 4: SAFE DRIVING PRACTICES

Safe driving practices are essential for reducing accidents, ensuring personal safety, and promoting efficient traffic flow in Kansas. This chapter explores defensive driving strategies, navigating adverse weather and low visibility conditions, and sharing the road responsibly with pedestrians, bicyclists, and motorcyclists.

Defensive Driving Strategies

Defensive driving involves anticipating potential hazards and taking proactive measures to avoid accidents. Key strategies include:

- Maintaining Awareness: Stay alert and aware of your surroundings at all times. Scan the road ahead, check mirrors frequently, and anticipate potential hazards.

- Keeping a Safe Distance: Maintain a safe following distance behind other vehicles to allow enough time to react and stop if necessary. Use the "two-second rule" under normal conditions, and increase distance in adverse weather or heavy traffic.

- Avoiding Distractions: Minimize distractions such as texting, eating, or adjusting controls while driving. Focus on the task of driving and remain attentive to changing road conditions.

- Being Courteous: Yield the right-of-way when required, signal intentions clearly, and avoid aggressive driving behaviors such as tailgating or excessive speeding.

By practicing defensive driving techniques, drivers can reduce the likelihood of collisions, protect themselves and others on the road, and contribute to overall traffic safety.

Driving in Adverse Conditions (Weather, Low Visibility)

Kansas experiences a variety of weather conditions throughout the year, including snow, ice, rain, and fog. When driving in adverse conditions:

- Reducing Speed: Slow down to maintain better control of the vehicle and increase stopping distances. Adjust your driving speed according to road conditions and visibility.

- Using Headlights: Turn on headlights in low light conditions, such as rain, fog, or dusk, to increase visibility to other drivers.

- Avoiding Sudden Maneuvers: Steer and brake gently to avoid skidding or losing control of the vehicle. Use caution on bridges and overpasses, as they freeze before other road surfaces.

- Monitoring Weather Reports: Check weather forecasts before traveling and consider delaying trips if severe weather is expected.

Adapting driving behavior to adverse weather conditions is crucial for preventing accidents and ensuring personal safety while on the road.

Sharing the Road with Pedestrians, Bicyclists, and Motorcycles

Sharing the road responsibly with vulnerable road users requires drivers to:

- Yield to Pedestrians: Always yield the right-of-way to pedestrians in crosswalks and at intersections. Be prepared to stop and allow pedestrians to cross safely.

- Giving Space to Cyclists: Leave at least three feet of space when passing bicyclists. Be aware of cyclists' movements and yield to them when turning or merging.

- Being Mindful of Motorcyclists: Check blind spots and mirrors carefully for motorcycles, which can be harder to see than other vehicles. Allow extra space and avoid sudden movements that may startle riders.

- Respecting Shared Spaces: Be patient and respectful when sharing roadways, paths, and lanes with pedestrians, bicyclists, and motorcyclists.

By adopting a mindset of mutual respect and vigilance, drivers can enhance safety for all road users and contribute to a harmonious transportation environment in Kansas.

Practicing defensive driving, navigating adverse conditions with caution, and sharing the road responsibly with pedestrians, bicyclists, and motorcyclists are essential components of safe driving practices in Kansas. By prioritizing safety, drivers can help reduce accidents and ensure a safer and more enjoyable driving experience for everyone.

Exam questions

1. Question: What is the primary goal of defensive driving?
   A) Speeding through traffic lights
   B) Anticipating potential hazards
   C) Racing with other vehicles
   D) Using the horn frequently

Correct Answer: B) Anticipating potential hazards

2. Question: What is a key aspect of maintaining safe following distance while driving?

A) Tailgating the vehicle in front

B) Using the "two-second rule"

C) Changing lanes frequently

D) Ignoring traffic signals

Correct Answer: B) Using the "two-second rule"

3. Question: Why is it important to minimize distractions while driving?

A) To save fuel

B) To avoid parking tickets

C) To maintain focus on driving tasks

D) To increase engine performance

Correct Answer: C) To maintain focus on driving tasks

4. Question: When should drivers turn on their headlights in adverse weather conditions?
A) Only during heavy rain
B) Only during nighttime hours
C) During rain, fog, or low light conditions
D) Never, as it can blind other drivers

Correct Answer: C) During rain, fog, or low light conditions

5. Question: What precaution should drivers take on bridges and overpasses during winter weather?

A) Drive faster to maintain control

B) Avoid using headlights

C) Steer and brake gently

D) Ignore warning signs

Correct Answer: C) Steer and brake gently

6. Question: What is the minimum space drivers should leave when passing bicyclists in Kansas?

A) One foot

B) Two feet

C) Three feet

D) Four feet

Correct Answer: C) Three feet

7. Question: How should drivers interact with pedestrians at crosswalks in Kansas?

A) Honk to alert pedestrians

B) Speed up to clear the crosswalk quickly

C) Yield the right-of-way and allow pedestrians to cross safely

D) Ignore pedestrians and proceed

Correct Answer: C) Yield the right-of-way and allow pedestrians to cross safely

8. Question: What should drivers do when approaching a motorcyclist in Kansas?

A) Change lanes without signaling

B) Check mirrors and blind spots carefully

C) Tailgate to urge them to go faster

D) Overtake them quickly

Correct Answer: B) Check mirrors and blind spots carefully

9. Question: How can drivers prepare for driving in adverse weather conditions?

  A) By ignoring weather forecasts

  B) By driving at maximum speed

  C) By increasing following distance

  D) By turning off headlights

Correct Answer: C) By increasing following distance

10. Question: What does defensive driving involve?

  A) Ignoring traffic signs

    B) Anticipating potential hazards and planning responses

  C) Speeding through intersections

  D) Using the horn frequently

Correct Answer: B) Anticipating potential hazards and planning responses

CHAPTER 5: SPECIAL DRIVING SITUATIONS

Driving in special situations requires heightened awareness and adherence to specific rules to ensure safety for all road users. This chapter explores driving in work zones and construction areas, navigating school zones and school buses, and approaching emergency vehicles and roadside assistance scenarios.

Driving in Work Zones and Construction Areas

Work zones and construction areas present unique challenges for drivers, including reduced speeds, lane closures, and the presence of construction workers and equipment. Tips for navigating these areas safely include:

- Reduced Speed: Obey posted speed limits within work zones to protect workers and maintain safety.

- Following Signs and Signals: Pay close attention to signs, signals, and flaggers directing traffic within construction zones.

- Lane Changes and Merging: Merge early when lane closures are indicated and be prepared for sudden changes in traffic patterns.

- Patience and Alertness: Remain patient and alert, expecting unexpected maneuvers from other drivers and construction vehicles.

Adhering to these guidelines helps prevent accidents and ensures the safety of both drivers and construction personnel.

Navigating School Zones and School Buses

School zones and school buses require extra caution to protect children and comply with traffic laws:

- Reduced Speed Limits: Observe reduced speed limits in school zones during specified hours when children are present.

- Stopping for School Buses: Stop and wait when a school bus displays flashing red lights and extends its stop arm, indicating children are entering or exiting the bus.

- Crossing Guards: Yield to crossing guards assisting children at crosswalks near schools.

- Awareness and Vigilance: Watch for children walking or biking to school, especially in residential areas and near bus stops.

Respecting these rules ensures the safety of young pedestrians and promotes a secure environment around schools.

Approaching Emergency Vehicles and Roadside Assistance

Approaching emergency vehicles and roadside assistance scenes requires immediate attention and compliance with traffic laws:

- Move Over Law: Kansas law requires drivers to move over one lane, if safe to do so, when approaching stationary emergency vehicles with flashing lights activated.

- Reduced Speed: Slow down and proceed with caution when passing emergency scenes or roadside assistance vehicles stopped on the shoulder.

- Avoiding Distractions: Focus on the road ahead and avoid distractions to maintain awareness of emergency vehicles and personnel.

- Clearing the Area Promptly: Once clear of the emergency scene, resume normal driving speed while remaining vigilant for other potential hazards.

By understanding and following these guidelines, drivers contribute to the safety of emergency responders and fellow motorists during critical situations.

Navigating special driving situations such as work zones, school zones, and emergency scenes requires vigilance, adherence to traffic laws, and respect for road conditions and other users. By practicing these principles, drivers enhance safety and promote responsible driving behavior on Kansas roadways.

Exam questions

1. Question: What should drivers do when approaching a work zone in Kansas?
   A) Increase speed to clear the area quickly
   B) Obey posted speed limits and signs

C) Ignore construction workers directing traffic

D) Drive in any available lane

Correct Answer: B) Obey posted speed limits and signs

2. Question: How should drivers navigate lane closures in work zones?

A) Merge early when possible

B) Speed through the closures

C) Change lanes abruptly

D) Drive in the closed lanes

Correct Answer: A) Merge early when possible

3. Question: When must drivers reduce speed in school zones in Kansas?

A) During nighttime hours only

B) On weekends and holidays

C) When children are present

D) Only during school recess periods

Correct Answer: C) When children are present

4. Question: What should drivers do when a school bus displays flashing red lights and an extended stop arm in Kansas?

A) Continue driving at the same speed

B) Pass the bus quickly

C) Stop and wait until the lights stop flashing and the arm retracts

D) Honk to alert children

Correct Answer: C) Stop and wait until the lights stop flashing and the arm retracts

5. Question: What is the Move Over Law in Kansas regarding emergency vehicles?

A) Drivers must move over one lane, if safe to do so, when approaching stationary emergency vehicles with flashing lights activated

B) Drivers must move over two lanes regardless of traffic conditions

C) Drivers must speed up to clear the area quickly

D) Drivers must ignore emergency vehicles on the road

Correct Answer: A) Drivers must move over one lane, if safe to do so, when approaching stationary emergency vehicles with flashing lights activated

6. Question: How should drivers approach a roadside assistance scene in Kansas?

A) Speed through the scene to avoid delays

B) Slow down and proceed with caution

C) Use hazard lights to warn others

D) Honk to alert assistance personnel

Correct Answer: B) Slow down and proceed with caution

7. Question: What is the primary purpose of reduced speed limits in work zones and school zones?

A) To increase fuel efficiency

B) To protect workers and children

C) To test vehicle brakes

D) To avoid traffic congestion

Correct Answer: B) To protect workers and children

8. Question: Why should drivers remain patient and alert in work zones?
   A) To race with other vehicles
   B) To increase travel time
   C) To anticipate unexpected maneuvers
   D) To ignore construction signs

   Correct Answer: C) To anticipate unexpected maneuvers

9. Question: What should drivers do when approaching a crossing guard near a school in Kansas?
   A) Speed up to clear the intersection quickly
   B) Yield to the crossing guard and children

C) Ignore the crossing guard's signals

D) Turn off headlights

Correct Answer: B) Yield to the crossing guard and children

10. Question: How can drivers promote safety when sharing the road with bicycles near school zones?

A) Honk to alert cyclists

B) Pass closely to show concern

C) Leave at least three feet of space when passing

D) Ignore cyclists on the road

Correct Answer: C) Leave at least three feet of space when passing

CHAPTER 6: DRIVER RESPONSIBILITIES AND LEGAL OBLIGATIONS

Understanding driver responsibilities and legal obligations is crucial for maintaining safety on Kansas roads and complying with state laws. This chapter covers insurance requirements and consequences, DUI laws, penalties, and consequences, as well as reporting accidents and filing claims.

Insurance Requirements and Consequences

In Kansas, drivers must comply with specific insurance requirements to legally operate a vehicle on public roads:

- Minimum Liability Coverage: Drivers must carry liability insurance that meets or exceeds the state's minimum requirements. This coverage includes bodily injury liability per person and per accident, as well as property damage liability.

- Proof of Insurance: Drivers must carry proof of insurance in their vehicles at all times. Proof of insurance can be in the form of an insurance card or electronic proof.

- Consequences of Non-Compliance: Failure to maintain proper insurance coverage can result in fines, license suspension, vehicle registration suspension, and other legal penalties. It is essential to ensure continuous coverage to comply with state law and protect oneself from financial liabilities in case of an accident.

Understanding and maintaining adequate insurance coverage not only fulfills legal obligations but also provides financial protection in the event of a collision or other covered incidents.

DUI Laws, Penalties, and Consequences

Driving under the influence (DUI) of alcohol or drugs is a serious offense in Kansas, with strict laws and severe penalties:

- Legal Blood Alcohol Concentration (BAC) Limit: The legal BAC limit in Kansas is 0.08% for drivers aged 21 and older. For drivers under 21, any detectable amount of alcohol in their system constitutes a violation.

- Penalties: Penalties for DUI convictions may include fines, license suspension or revocation, mandatory alcohol education or treatment programs, community service, and even imprisonment for repeat offenses or aggravated circumstances.

- Implied Consent: Kansas operates under an implied consent law, meaning drivers implicitly agree to submit to a chemical test (breath, blood, or urine) to determine BAC if lawfully arrested for DUI. Refusal to submit to such tests can lead to administrative penalties, including license suspension.

Understanding DUI laws, exercising responsible drinking habits, and avoiding impaired driving are critical to promoting safety and compliance with Kansas traffic laws.

Reporting Accidents and Filing Claims

Prompt and accurate reporting of accidents and filing insurance claims are essential for resolving disputes and obtaining compensation for damages:

- Reporting Requirements: Drivers involved in accidents resulting in injury, death, or property damage exceeding a certain amount must immediately report the incident to law enforcement and, if necessary, file a written report with the Kansas Department of Revenue.

- Filing Insurance Claims: Drivers should notify their insurance company promptly after an accident to initiate the claims process. Provide accurate details of the incident, including the date, time, location, and description of damages or injuries sustained.

- Legal Considerations: Adhering to reporting requirements and properly documenting the accident scene can facilitate insurance claims processing and legal proceedings if disputes arise.

By understanding insurance requirements, DUI laws, penalties, and consequences, as well as proper procedures for reporting accidents and filing claims, drivers in Kansas can fulfill their legal obligations, protect themselves from financial liabilities, and contribute to safer roadways for all users. Continued education and compliance with these laws are essential for responsible and lawful driving practices.

Exam questions

1. Question: What is the minimum liability insurance coverage required for drivers in Kansas?

   A) Coverage for property damage only

   B) Coverage for bodily injury liability per accident

   C) Coverage for medical payments only

   D) Coverage for personal belongings

   Correct Answer: B) Coverage for bodily injury liability per accident

2. Question: What must drivers carry as proof of insurance in Kansas?

A) A valid driver's license

B) Proof of vehicle registration

C) Proof of vehicle inspection

D) Proof of insurance card or electronic proof

Correct Answer: D) Proof of insurance card or electronic proof

3. Question: What are the potential consequences of driving without insurance in Kansas?

A) No consequences

B) Fine and license suspension

C) Community service only

D) Traffic school enrollment

Correct Answer: B) Fine and license suspension

4. Question: What is the legal Blood Alcohol Concentration (BAC) limit for drivers aged 21 and older in Kansas?

   A) 0.05%

   B) 0.08%

   C) 0.10%

   D) 0.15%

Correct Answer: B) 0.08%

5. Question: What penalties might drivers face for a DUI conviction in Kansas?

   A) Fine and warning

   B) License suspension, fines, and possible imprisonment

   C) Verbal warning only

D) Community service only

Correct Answer: B) License suspension, fines, and possible imprisonment

6. Question: Under Kansas's implied consent law, what happens if a driver refuses to submit to a chemical test (breath, blood, or urine) after a lawful DUI arrest?
   A) No consequences
   B) Reduced fines
   C) License suspension
   D) Verbal warning only

Correct Answer: C) License suspension

7. Question: When must drivers report an accident to law enforcement in Kansas?
   A) Only if injuries are involved

B) Only if property damage exceeds $1,000

C) Immediately if injuries, death, or property damage over $1,000 occur

D) Within 24 hours regardless of damage or injuries

Correct Answer: C) Immediately if injuries, death, or property damage over $1,000 occur

8. Question: What should drivers do after being involved in an accident in Kansas to begin the insurance claims process?

A) Wait for the other party to file a report

B) Notify their insurance company promptly

C) Do nothing and wait for the police report

D) Contact the Department of Revenue

Correct Answer: B) Notify their insurance company promptly

9. Question: What legal considerations should drivers keep in mind when reporting accidents and filing claims in Kansas?
   A) Ignoring reporting requirements
   B) Providing inaccurate information
   C) Filing claims without proof of insurance
   D) Following reporting requirements and providing accurate details

Correct Answer: D) Following reporting requirements and providing accurate details

10. Question: Why is it important for drivers to understand insurance requirements, DUI

laws, and accident reporting procedures in Kansas?

A) To increase traffic congestion

B) To avoid financial penalties and legal consequences

C) To ignore road signs

D) To speed through intersections

Correct Answer: B) To avoid financial penalties and legal consequences

CHAPTER 7: VEHICLE OPERATION AND MAINTENANCE

Proper vehicle operation and maintenance are essential for ensuring safety, reliability, and longevity of vehicles on Kansas roads. This chapter covers vehicle safety inspections and requirements, basic vehicle maintenance tips, and handling emergencies and breakdowns effectively.

Vehicle Safety Inspections and Requirements

Regular safety inspections help ensure that vehicles are in proper working condition and meet state requirements:

- Inspection Frequency: Kansas requires vehicles to undergo safety inspections periodically, typically annually or biennially depending on the vehicle type and age.

- Components Checked: Inspections typically include checks on brakes, lights, tires, steering, suspension, exhaust system, and other essential safety features.

- Certification and Compliance: Vehicles that pass inspections receive certification, which is required for vehicle registration renewal. Non-compliance can result in fines or registration suspension.

Adhering to safety inspection requirements helps identify potential issues early and ensures vehicles are safe for operation on public roads.

Basic Vehicle Maintenance Tips

Routine maintenance helps maintain vehicle performance, reliability, and safety:

- Oil and Fluid Changes: Regularly change engine oil, transmission fluid, brake fluid, and coolant as recommended by the vehicle manufacturer.

- Tire Care: Check tire pressure regularly and inspect tread depth. Rotate tires as recommended to ensure even wear and better handling.

- Brake Maintenance: Monitor brake pads and discs for wear and replace them promptly if signs of wear are detected. Ensure brake fluid levels are adequate.

- Battery Care: Inspect the battery regularly for corrosion and ensure terminals are clean. Replace batteries as needed to prevent unexpected failures.

- Lights and Signals: Regularly check headlights, brake lights, turn signals, and hazard lights to ensure they are functioning properly.

By following these maintenance tips, drivers can reduce the risk of breakdowns and ensure their vehicles operate efficiently and safely.

Handling Emergencies and Breakdowns

Knowing how to respond to emergencies and breakdowns can prevent further damage and ensure safety:

- Safety First: Move the vehicle to a safe location away from traffic if possible. Use hazard lights to alert other drivers.

- Assess the Situation: Determine the nature of the problem (e.g., flat tire, overheating) and take appropriate action.

- Calling for Assistance: Contact roadside assistance or emergency services if needed. Be prepared to provide your location and details about the situation.

- Basic Repairs: Carry essential tools and supplies, such as a spare tire, jack, and tire iron, to handle minor repairs like changing a flat tire.

- Staying Informed: Understand basic troubleshooting steps for common issues and know when to seek professional assistance.

Being prepared for emergencies and conducting regular maintenance are essential practices for responsible vehicle ownership and safe driving in Kansas.

By understanding and implementing vehicle operation and maintenance practices, drivers can enhance safety, prolong vehicle life, and minimize the risk of accidents and breakdowns on Kansas roads. Regular inspections, proactive maintenance, and preparedness for emergencies contribute to a safer and more reliable driving experience for all motorists.

Exam Questions

1. Question: Why are regular safety inspections important for vehicles in Kansas?

   A) To increase vehicle registration fees

B) To ensure vehicles are in proper working condition

C) To avoid traffic tickets

D) To ignore vehicle maintenance

Correct Answer: B) To ensure vehicles are in proper working condition

2. Question: What components are typically checked during a vehicle safety inspection in Kansas?

A) Only engine oil

B) Brakes, lights, tires, and steering

C) Transmission fluid only

D) Horn and windshield wipers

Correct Answer: B) Brakes, lights, tires, and steering

3. Question: How often are vehicles in Kansas required to undergo safety inspections?

A) Every month

B) Biennially (every two years)

C) Quarterly

D) Annually

Correct Answer: D) Annually

4. Question: Why is it important to regularly change engine oil and fluids in a vehicle?

A) To increase vehicle weight

B) To reduce fuel efficiency

C) To maintain engine performance and longevity

D) To increase maintenance costs

Correct Answer: C) To maintain engine performance and longevity

5. Question: What should drivers check regularly to ensure tire safety?

   A) Tire pressure and tread depth

   B) Vehicle weight capacity

   C) Battery voltage

   D) Engine oil level

   Correct Answer: A) Tire pressure and tread depth

6. Question: How can drivers maintain brake safety in their vehicles?

   A) Never check brake pads

   B) Monitor brake pads for wear and replace them as needed

   C) Ignore brake fluid levels

D) Speed through intersections

Correct Answer: B) Monitor brake pads for wear and replace them as needed

7. Question: What should drivers do if they experience a breakdown on the road?

A) Continue driving to the nearest gas station

B) Move the vehicle to a safe location away from traffic

C) Immediately call roadside assistance

D) Honk the horn repeatedly

Correct Answer: B) Move the vehicle to a safe location away from traffic

8. Question: Why should drivers use hazard lights during a breakdown or emergency situation?

A) To signal a turn

B) To alert other drivers of a problem

C) To increase vehicle speed

D) To confuse other drivers

Correct Answer: B) To alert other drivers of a problem

9. Question: What should drivers carry to handle minor repairs during a breakdown?

A) Spare tire, jack, and tire iron

B) Spare engine

C) Spare windshield wipers

D) Spare fuel tank

Correct Answer: A) Spare tire, jack, and tire iron

10. Question: How can drivers prepare for emergencies and breakdowns?

   A) By ignoring vehicle maintenance

   B) By carrying essential tools and supplies

   C) By increasing vehicle speed

   D) By ignoring traffic signs

   Correct Answer: B) By carrying essential tools and supplies

CHAPTER 8: UNDERSTANDING ROAD SIGNS AND MARKINGS

Road signs and pavement markings play a critical role in guiding and regulating traffic flow, ensuring safety, and conveying important information to drivers on Kansas roads. This chapter explores the different types of road signs, pavement markings, and traffic signals, emphasizing their meanings and significance.

Regulatory, Warning, and Guide Signs

Road signs in Kansas are categorized into three main types: regulatory, warning, and guide signs.

- Regulatory Signs: These signs are essential for controlling and regulating the movement of traffic. They include speed limit signs, stop signs, yield signs, and signs indicating lane usage and turning regulations. Compliance with regulatory signs is mandatory and helps maintain order and safety on the road.

- Warning Signs: Warning signs alert drivers to potential hazards ahead, such as sharp curves, intersections, pedestrian crossings, and changes in road conditions like slippery surfaces or steep hills. These signs prepare drivers to adjust their speed or take necessary precautions to avoid accidents.

- Guide Signs: Guide signs provide directional and distance information, helping drivers navigate to destinations efficiently. Examples include route markers, highway exit signs, and signs indicating services such as rest areas, gas stations, and hospitals. Following guide signs ensures drivers stay on course and reach their destinations without confusion.

Understanding and obeying these signs are essential for safe and lawful driving practices in Kansas.

Pavement Markings and Their Meanings

Pavement markings complement road signs by providing additional guidance and information to drivers:

- Yellow and White Lines: Yellow lines typically separate traffic moving in opposite directions, while white lines separate traffic moving in the same direction. Dashed lines indicate passing zones, while solid lines indicate no passing zones or lane boundaries.

- Crosswalks and Stop Lines: Crosswalk markings indicate where pedestrians can safely cross the road, while stop lines indicate where drivers must stop at intersections or crosswalks.

- Arrows and Symbols: Arrows on the pavement direct traffic flow, indicating lane use or the direction vehicles should take at intersections. Symbols such as bicycle lanes or turning arrows provide specific instructions for drivers.

Understanding the meanings of pavement markings helps drivers navigate intersections, lanes, and roadways safely and efficiently.

Interpretation of Traffic Signals

Traffic signals control the flow of traffic at intersections and pedestrian crossings, promoting orderly movement and reducing the risk of collisions:

- Red, Yellow, and Green Lights: Red indicates stop, yellow indicates prepare to stop or proceed with caution, and green indicates go. Drivers must obey these signals to prevent accidents and ensure smooth traffic flow.

- Pedestrian Signals: Pedestrian signals indicate when it is safe for pedestrians to cross the street, synchronized with traffic lights to manage pedestrian and vehicle movements.

- Special Signals: Special signals such as railroad crossing signals or emergency vehicle preemption signals provide specific instructions that drivers must follow to ensure safety and compliance.

By understanding and respecting traffic signals, drivers contribute to safer roadways and reduce the likelihood of accidents caused by confusion or non-compliance.

Comprehensive knowledge of road signs, pavement markings, and traffic signals is crucial for safe and efficient driving in Kansas. By familiarizing themselves with these visual cues and following their instructions, drivers can navigate roadways confidently while promoting traffic safety for themselves and others.

Exam questions

1. Question: What type of road sign is indicated by a red circle with a white horizontal line inside?
   A) Regulatory sign
   B) Warning sign
   C) Guide sign
   D) Informational sign

Correct Answer: A) Regulatory sign

2. Question: What does a yellow diamond-shaped sign with black symbols or letters represent?

  A) A regulatory sign

  B) A warning sign

  C) A guide sign

  D) A speed limit sign

Correct Answer: B) A warning sign

3. Question: What do white lane markings on the pavement typically indicate?

  A) No passing zone

  B) Passing zone

  C) Stop line

  D) Pedestrian crosswalk

Correct Answer: A) No passing zone

4. Question: What do dashed yellow lines on the road indicate to drivers?

A) Passing zone

B) No passing zone

C) Stop line

D) Pedestrian crosswalk

Correct Answer: A) Passing zone

5. Question: What does a solid white line on the road indicate to drivers?

A) Passing zone

B) No passing zone

C) Stop line

D) Pedestrian crosswalk

Correct Answer: B) No passing zone

6. Question: What does a yellow line alongside a white line on the road indicate to drivers?

A) Passing zone

B) No passing zone

C) Two-way traffic

D) Construction zone

Correct Answer: C) Two-way traffic

7. Question: What does a red traffic light indicate to drivers?

A) Prepare to stop or proceed with caution

B) Go

C) Slow down

D) Stop

Correct Answer: D) Stop

8. Question: What should drivers do when approaching a flashing yellow traffic signal?

A) Speed up

B) Continue through the intersection with caution

C) Stop immediately

D) Make a U-turn

Correct Answer: B) Continue through the intersection with caution

9. Question: What does a pedestrian signal showing a white walking figure indicate to drivers?

A) Pedestrians should not cross

B) Pedestrians should cross with caution

C) Vehicles should proceed without stopping

D) Vehicles should prepare to stop

Correct Answer: C) Vehicles should proceed without stopping

10. Question: What do railroad crossing signals indicate to drivers?

A) Slow down

B) Proceed with caution

C) Stop if a train is approaching

D) Ignore the signal

Correct Answer: C) Stop if a train is approaching

CHAPTER 9: DRIVER'S LICENSE APPLICATION AND TESTING

Obtaining a driver's license in Kansas involves passing both a written knowledge test and a road skills test. This chapter provides comprehensive guidance on preparing for these tests, along with tips, strategies, common mistakes, and how to avoid them.

Preparing for the Written Knowledge Test

The written knowledge test assesses understanding of traffic laws, road signs, and safe driving practices:

- Study Materials: Utilize the Kansas Driver's Handbook and practice tests available to familiarize yourself with relevant topics and questions.

- Key Topics: Focus on regulatory signs, traffic signals, right-of-way rules, speed limits, and road safety guidelines outlined in the handbook.

- Practice Makes Perfect: Take multiple practice tests to gauge your knowledge and identify areas needing further review.

By thoroughly preparing and studying the materials provided, you can increase your confidence and readiness for the written knowledge test.

Tips and Strategies for the Road Skills Test

The road skills test evaluates practical driving skills and adherence to traffic laws:

- Practice Driving: Gain hands-on experience behind the wheel under various conditions, including different weather and traffic scenarios.

- Review Driving Maneuvers: Practice parking, turning, lane changes, and obeying traffic signs and signals.

- Mock Tests: Schedule practice sessions with a licensed driver or driving instructor to simulate test conditions and receive constructive feedback.

Preparing adequately and familiarizing yourself with the test route and requirements will enhance your performance during the road skills test.

Common Mistakes and How to Avoid Them

Identifying and avoiding common mistakes can improve your chances of passing both tests:

- Failure to Yield: Understand right-of-way rules and yield to pedestrians and other vehicles as required.

- Speeding and Unsafe Maneuvers: Adhere to posted speed limits and avoid aggressive or unsafe driving behaviors.

- Improper Parking and Turns: Practice precise parking techniques and execute turns safely, using signals as required.

By learning from these mistakes and practicing diligently, you can demonstrate safe driving habits and increase your likelihood of passing the tests successfully.

Achieving a driver's license in Kansas requires preparation, practice, and adherence to traffic laws and safety guidelines. By following the guidance provided in this chapter, you can approach the written knowledge test and road skills test with confidence, avoid common pitfalls, and demonstrate your readiness to drive safely on Kansas roadways.

1. Question: What should you study to prepare for the written knowledge test in Kansas?

A) Traffic fines and penalties

B) Kansas Driver's Handbook and practice tests

C) Vehicle registration procedures

D) Local weather forecasts

Correct Answer: B) Kansas Driver's Handbook and practice tests

2. Question: What does the written knowledge test in Kansas assess?

A) Practical driving skills

B) Understanding of traffic laws and road signs

C) Vehicle maintenance knowledge

D) Knowledge of local landmarks

Correct Answer: B) Understanding of traffic laws and road signs

3. Question: What is an effective strategy for preparing for the road skills test?
   A) Avoiding practice drives
   B) Memorizing road maps
   C) Practicing driving under different conditions
   D) Studying traffic statistics

Correct Answer: C) Practicing driving under different conditions

4. Question: What should you do to simulate test conditions for the road skills test?
   A) Take a break from driving

B) Practice with a licensed driver or instructor

C) Drive at night only

D) Ignore traffic signs

Correct Answer: B) Practice with a licensed driver or instructor

5. Question: What common mistake should you avoid during the road skills test related to turns?

A) Not using turn signals

B) Making turns too slowly

C) Making turns too quickly

D) Ignoring stop signs

Correct Answer: A) Not using turn signals

6. Question: During the road skills test, what should you do when approaching a pedestrian crosswalk?

   A) Speed up to cross quickly

   B) Stop and yield to pedestrians

   C) Drive through without slowing down

   D) Sound the horn to alert pedestrians

   Correct Answer: B) Stop and yield to pedestrians

7. Question: What is one area commonly tested during the road skills test related to parking?

   A) Parking in no-parking zones

   B) Parallel parking and angle parking

   C) Ignoring parking regulations

   D) Parking on sidewalks

Correct Answer: B) Parallel parking and angle parking

8. Question: What should you do if you make a mistake during the road skills test?

A) Repeat the mistake to demonstrate consistency

B) Acknowledge the mistake and continue driving safely

C) Stop and exit the vehicle

D) Speed away to avoid attention

Correct Answer: B) Acknowledge the mistake and continue driving safely

9. Question: What should you demonstrate during the road skills test related to speed limits?

A) Exceeding posted speed limits

B) Driving at or below posted speed limits

C) Ignoring speed limits

D) Racing other vehicles

Correct Answer: B) Driving at or below posted speed limits

10. Question: What is the purpose of practicing multiple mock tests before the written knowledge test?

A) To memorize answers

B) To gauge knowledge and identify areas needing review

C) To ignore traffic laws

D) To rush through the test

Correct Answer: B) To gauge knowledge and identify areas needing review

CHAPTER 10: ADVANCED DRIVING TECHNIQUES

Advanced driving techniques go beyond basic skills, focusing on strategies to enhance safety, efficiency, and confidence in various challenging driving conditions. This chapter explores defensive driving in high-traffic areas, navigating highways and freeways, and mastering advanced maneuvers with heightened situational awareness.

Defensive Driving in High-Traffic Areas

Driving defensively involves anticipating potential hazards and reacting appropriately to prevent accidents:

- Maintaining Safe Following Distance: Keep a safe distance from the vehicle ahead to allow time for braking and maneuvering.

- Using Mirrors and Blind Spot Checks: Regularly check mirrors and blind spots to monitor surrounding traffic and potential hazards.

- Predicting Other Drivers' Actions: Anticipate actions of other drivers by observing their behavior and signals.

- Minimizing Distractions: Focus on driving and avoid distractions such as mobile phones or adjusting radio settings.

By adopting defensive driving techniques, drivers can mitigate risks and respond effectively to unexpected situations in congested traffic environments.

Driving on Highways and Freeways

Navigating highways and freeways requires specific skills and awareness:

- Entering and Exiting Safely: Use acceleration lanes to match the speed of highway traffic when entering. Signal early and merge smoothly when exiting.

- Maintaining Consistent Speed: Adhere to posted speed limits and maintain a steady speed to enhance traffic flow and safety.

- Lane Changing and Merging: Use turn signals and check mirrors and blind spots before changing lanes or merging into traffic.

- Managing Interchanges and Exits: Understand signage for interchanges and exits, preparing well in advance to avoid last-minute maneuvers.

Mastering highway driving involves confidence, patience, and adherence to traffic laws and etiquette for safe travel.

Advanced Maneuvers and Situational Awareness

Enhancing driving skills includes mastering advanced maneuvers and maintaining situational awareness:

- Parallel Parking: Practice precise parking techniques in tight spaces, using mirrors and backup cameras effectively.

- Emergency Maneuvers: Learn techniques for evasive maneuvers, such as sudden braking or swerving, to avoid collisions.

- Handling Adverse Conditions: Navigate adverse weather conditions like rain, snow, or fog by reducing speed and increasing following distance.

- Monitoring Traffic Patterns: Continuously assess traffic flow, road conditions, and potential hazards to adjust driving strategy accordingly.

By honing advanced driving skills and maintaining heightened awareness, drivers can navigate complex road scenarios confidently and safely.

Advanced driving techniques encompass defensive strategies, highway navigation skills, and mastery of advanced maneuvers with heightened situational awareness. By practicing these techniques and maintaining a proactive approach to safety, drivers can reduce risks, enhance driving proficiency, and contribute to safer roadways for themselves and others. Understanding the principles outlined in this chapter prepares drivers to handle diverse driving challenges effectively and responsibly.

Exam questions

1. Question: What is a key principle of defensive driving in high-traffic areas?

  A) Tailgating other vehicles

  B) Using mobile phones while driving

  C) Maintaining a safe following distance

  D) Ignoring road signs

    Correct Answer: C) Maintaining a safe following distance

2. Question: How can drivers enhance situational awareness on highways?

  A) Speeding up to pass slower vehicles

  B) Avoiding the use of mirrors

    C) Monitoring traffic patterns and road conditions

  D) Driving with distractions

Correct Answer: C) Monitoring traffic patterns and road conditions

3. Question: What should drivers do when entering a freeway from an on-ramp?
   A) Merge into traffic without signaling
    B) Match the speed of highway traffic using the acceleration lane
    C) Slow down abruptly to find a gap in traffic
   D) Exit the freeway immediately

    Correct Answer: B) Match the speed of highway traffic using the acceleration lane ·

4. Question: How can drivers safely navigate highway exits?
    A) Brake suddenly upon reaching the exit ramp

B) Signal early and merge smoothly into the exit lane

C) Change lanes without checking mirrors or blind spots

D) Ignore exit signs and continue driving

Correct Answer: B) Signal early and merge smoothly into the exit lane

5. Question: What is an important consideration when changing lanes on a freeway?

A) Changing lanes without signaling

B) Cutting off other vehicles

C) Using turn signals and checking mirrors and blind spots

D) Speeding up to block other vehicles

Correct Answer: C) Using turn signals and checking mirrors and blind spots

6. Question: What should drivers do to master parallel parking?

A) Ignore surrounding vehicles

B) Practice precise parking techniques using mirrors and backup cameras

C) Park at an angle to block other vehicles

D) Park on sidewalks

Correct Answer: B) Practice precise parking techniques using mirrors and backup cameras

7. Question: How should drivers approach emergency maneuvers?

A) Avoid braking suddenly or swerving to avoid collisions

B) Practice swerving abruptly in traffic

C) Ignore emergency vehicles

D) Follow other vehicles closely

Correct Answer: A) Avoid braking suddenly or swerving to avoid collisions

8. Question: What should drivers do when encountering adverse weather conditions?

A) Increase speed to reach the destination faster

B) Reduce speed and increase following distance

C) Turn off headlights to save battery

D) Ignore road conditions

Correct Answer: B) Reduce speed and increase following distance

9. Question: Why is maintaining consistent speed important on highways?

   A) To exceed speed limits

   B) To enhance traffic flow and safety

   C) To ignore traffic signals

   D) To race other vehicles

   Correct Answer: B) To enhance traffic flow and safety

10. Question: How can drivers improve their highway navigation skills?

   A) By ignoring road signs

   B) By driving slowly in the left lane

     C) By planning routes and exits in advance

   D) By not using turn signals

Correct Answer: C) By planning routes and exits in advance

CHAPTER 11: ENVIRONMENTAL CONSIDERATIONS

In recent years, environmental awareness has become increasingly important in all aspects of daily life, including driving practices. This chapter delves into eco-friendly driving practices, understanding vehicle emissions, and the impact of driving choices on the environment.

Eco-Friendly Driving Practices

Eco-friendly driving focuses on minimizing the environmental impact of vehicles through efficient use of fuel and reduction of emissions:

- Smooth Driving: Avoid sudden acceleration and braking, which can waste fuel and increase emissions.

- Maintaining Proper Tire Pressure: Properly inflated tires reduce fuel consumption and improve vehicle efficiency.

- Reducing Idling Time: Turn off the engine when parked or waiting to reduce unnecessary emissions.

- Using Cruise Control: On highways, cruise control helps maintain a consistent speed, optimizing fuel efficiency.

- Choosing Fuel-Efficient Vehicles: Select vehicles with high fuel economy ratings and consider hybrid or electric models for lower emissions.

Adopting these practices not only reduces fuel costs but also contributes to cleaner air and a healthier environment.

Understanding Vehicle Emissions

Vehicle emissions consist of pollutants released during fuel combustion, impacting air quality and contributing to climate change:

- Types of Pollutants: Common emissions include carbon dioxide (CO_2), nitrogen oxides (NO_x), particulate matter (PM), and hydrocarbons (HC).

- Environmental Impact: These pollutants contribute to smog formation, respiratory illnesses, and global warming.

- Emission Standards: Governments enforce emission standards to regulate vehicle emissions and promote cleaner technologies.

By understanding vehicle emissions and their effects, drivers can make informed choices to minimize environmental impact.

Impact of Driving Choices on the Environment

Driving habits and vehicle choices significantly influence environmental outcomes:

- Fuel Type and Efficiency: Opt for cleaner-burning fuels and vehicles with higher fuel efficiency ratings.

- Transportation Alternatives: Consider carpooling, public transportation, biking, or walking to reduce vehicle use and emissions.

- Maintenance Practices: Regular vehicle maintenance, such as tune-ups and emissions inspections, ensures optimal performance and reduces emissions.

- Educational Awareness: Promote environmental awareness among drivers and communities to encourage sustainable driving practices.

Each individual's driving choices contribute to collective efforts in environmental conservation and sustainability. By adopting eco-friendly practices and making informed decisions, drivers can minimize their carbon footprint and preserve natural resources for future generations.

Environmental considerations in driving encompass eco-friendly practices, understanding vehicle emissions, and the impact of driving choices on the environment. By integrating these principles into daily driving routines, drivers can contribute to cleaner air, reduced greenhouse gas emissions, and a sustainable future. This chapter emphasizes the role of responsible driving behaviors in mitigating environmental impact and fostering environmental stewardship within communities.

Exam questions

1. Question: What is a key eco-friendly driving practice to reduce fuel consumption and emissions?
   A) Sudden acceleration and braking
   B) Maintaining proper tire pressure
   C) Keeping the engine idling when parked
   D) Using high-octane fuel

   Correct Answer: B) Maintaining proper tire pressure

2. Question: How can using cruise control on highways contribute to eco-friendly driving?

A) Increases fuel efficiency

B) Decreases fuel efficiency

C) Reduces vehicle emissions

D) Causes engine overheating

Correct Answer: A) Increases fuel efficiency

3. Question: What are common types of vehicle emissions that impact air quality?

A) Oxygen and nitrogen

B) Carbon dioxide and water vapor

C) Nitrogen oxides and particulate matter

D) Hydrogen and helium

Correct Answer: C) Nitrogen oxides and particulate matter

4. Question: How do vehicle emissions contribute to environmental issues?

A) Improve air quality

B) Reduce global warming

C) Contribute to smog formation and climate change

D) Enhance biodiversity

Correct Answer: C) Contribute to smog formation and climate change

5. Question: What role do emission standards play in regulating vehicle emissions?

A) Encouraging higher emissions

B) Promoting cleaner technologies

C) Ignoring environmental impacts

D) Increasing pollution levels

Correct Answer: B) Promoting cleaner technologies

6. Question: What impact do driving habits and vehicle choices have on the environment?

A) No impact on emissions

B) Reduce carbon footprint

C) Increase environmental awareness

D) Deplete natural resources

Correct Answer: B) Reduce carbon footprint

7. Question: Why is regular vehicle maintenance important for reducing emissions?

A) Increases fuel consumption

B) Enhances vehicle performance

C) Causes higher emissions

D) Ignores environmental impact

Correct Answer: B) Enhances vehicle performance

8. Question: What transportation alternatives can help reduce vehicle emissions?

A) Carpooling, public transportation, biking, or walking

B) Increasing vehicle use

C) Using high-emission vehicles only

D) Ignoring fuel efficiency

Correct Answer: A) Carpooling, public transportation, biking, or walking

9. Question: How does promoting environmental awareness among drivers benefit communities?

A) Increases pollution levels

B) Encourages sustainable driving practices

C) Ignores climate change

D) Decreases environmental impact

Correct Answer: B) Encourages sustainable driving practices

10. Question: What is the primary goal of adopting eco-friendly driving practices?

A) Maximizing fuel consumption

B) Minimizing vehicle efficiency

C) Reducing environmental impact

D) Ignoring emission standards

Correct Answer: C) Reducing environmental impact

CHAPTER 12: EMERGENCY PROCEDURES AND CRISIS MANAGEMENT

Emergencies on the road can occur suddenly and require quick, informed responses to ensure safety for everyone involved. This chapter covers essential techniques for handling vehicle emergencies, dealing with roadside assistance and emergency services, and crisis management with effective de-escalation techniques.

Handling Vehicle Emergencies

Encountering vehicle emergencies such as brake failure or tire blowouts demands swift and effective action to mitigate risks:

- Brake Failure: If brakes fail, remain calm and try pumping the brake pedal to build up pressure. Use the emergency/parking brake gradually to slow down and safely pull over.

- Tire Blowouts: When a tire blows out, avoid sudden steering maneuvers. Keep a firm grip on the steering wheel, gradually reduce speed, and pull over to a safe location away from traffic.

- Engine Failure: If the engine fails, steer the vehicle to the side of the road while maintaining control. Use hazard lights to signal other drivers and seek assistance.

- Handling Fire: In case of a vehicle fire, safely pull over, turn off the engine, and evacuate all occupants. Use a fire extinguisher if available and call emergency services immediately.

Preparing for these emergencies includes regular vehicle maintenance, carrying essential tools like a spare tire and jack, and knowing how to react calmly under pressure.

Dealing with Roadside Assistance and Emergency Services

Knowing how to access and interact with roadside assistance and emergency services is crucial for prompt resolution of issues:

- Contact Information: Keep emergency contact numbers handy, including roadside assistance services and local emergency services.

- Effective Communication: Clearly communicate your location, vehicle description, and the nature of the emergency to dispatchers or responders.

- Follow Instructions: Follow instructions from emergency responders or roadside assistance providers carefully to ensure your safety and the swift resolution of the situation.

- Roadside Safety: When awaiting assistance, position your vehicle safely off the road, activate hazard lights, and use reflective triangles or flares if available to alert other drivers.

Understanding procedures for obtaining help efficiently can minimize delays and ensure effective resolution of roadside emergencies.

Crisis Management and De-escalation Techniques

Encountering stressful situations on the road, such as accidents or disputes, requires effective crisis management and de-escalation strategies:

- Stay Calm: Maintain composure and avoid escalating the situation through aggressive behavior or language.

- Listen Actively: Listen to others involved in the crisis to understand their concerns and perspectives.

- Offer Assistance: If safe to do so, provide assistance to others involved in the crisis, such as offering first aid or contacting emergency services.

- Resolve Conflict: Use respectful communication and negotiation skills to resolve conflicts peacefully and responsibly.

Developing these skills contributes to safer road environments and fosters positive interactions during challenging situations.

Emergency procedures and crisis management skills are essential for all drivers to ensure safety and effective response during unexpected situations on the road. By preparing for vehicle emergencies, knowing how to access roadside assistance and emergency services, and mastering crisis de-escalation techniques, drivers can mitigate risks, promote road safety, and contribute to a supportive driving community. This chapter emphasizes the importance of proactive preparation and responsible behavior in managing emergencies effectively.

Exam questions

1. Question: What should you do in the event of brake failure while driving?
   A) Accelerate to regain control
   B) Pump the brake pedal to build pressure
   C) Ignore the issue and continue driving
   D) Use cruise control to stabilize speed

   Correct Answer: B) Pump the brake pedal to build pressure

2. Question: How should you handle a tire blowout while driving?

A) Make sudden steering maneuvers

B) Maintain a firm grip on the steering wheel

C) Ignore the blowout and continue driving

D) Speed up to stabilize the vehicle

Correct Answer: B) Maintain a firm grip on the steering wheel

3. Question: What is a critical step when experiencing engine failure on the road?

A) Immediately exit the vehicle

B) Use hazard lights to signal other drivers

C) Accelerate to reach the nearest service station

D) Ignore the issue and wait for help

Correct Answer: B) Use hazard lights to signal other drivers

4. Question: How should you respond to a vehicle fire?

A) Stay inside the vehicle until help arrives

B) Use a fire extinguisher to put out the fire

C) Speed away from the fire scene

D) Ignore the fire and continue driving

Correct Answer: B) Use a fire extinguisher to put out the fire

5. Question: What information should you provide when contacting roadside assistance?

A) Vehicle description and driver's license number

B) Your favorite color and hobby

C) Your home address and phone number

D) Location, vehicle description, and nature of the emergency

Correct Answer: D) Location, vehicle description, and nature of the emergency

6. Question: How can you ensure your safety while awaiting roadside assistance?

A) Keep the vehicle running with air conditioning on

B) Park in the middle of the road

C) Use hazard lights and reflective triangles or flares

D) Ignore passing vehicles

Correct Answer: C) Use hazard lights and reflective triangles or flares

7. Question: What is an essential skill in crisis management during road incidents?

A) Engaging in aggressive behavior

B) Listening actively to understand concerns

C) Ignoring others' perspectives

D) Speeding away from the scene

Correct Answer: B) Listening actively to understand concerns

8. Question: How should you approach resolving conflicts during road incidents?

A) Use respectful communication and negotiation skills

B) Avoid communication altogether

C) Yell loudly to intimidate others

D) Ignore the conflict and leave the scene

Correct Answer: A) Use respectful communication and negotiation skills

9. Question: Why is it important to stay calm during crisis situations on the road?

A) To escalate tensions

B) To cause accidents

C) To maintain composure and make rational decisions

D) To ignore safety protocols

Correct Answer: C) To maintain composure and make rational decisions

10. Question: What role do emergency services play in managing road incidents?

A) They contribute to road congestion

B) They delay response times

C) They provide timely assistance and ensure safety

D) They ignore emergency calls

Correct Answer: C) They provide timely assistance and ensure safety

CONCLUSION

In conclusion, the Driver's License Handbook serves as an essential guide for individuals embarking on the journey of becoming licensed drivers. Throughout its chapters, readers have explored fundamental traffic laws, road signs, safe driving practices, and emergency procedures necessary for navigating the roadways responsibly.

This handbook not only equips readers with practical knowledge but also emphasizes the importance of adherence to regulations, respect for road safety, and consideration for fellow road users. By mastering the information presented here, drivers can contribute to creating safer and more efficient transportation environments for themselves and their communities.

As drivers continue to apply the principles learned from this handbook, they are encouraged to prioritize ongoing education, practice safe driving habits, and stay updated on evolving traffic laws and technologies. By doing so, they not only enhance their driving skills but also play an active role in promoting a culture of safety and responsibility on the roads.

Whether preparing for the written knowledge test, seeking to refresh driving knowledge, or aiming to foster a deeper understanding of road rules and procedures, this handbook serves as a comprehensive resource. It is designed to empower drivers with the confidence and competence needed to navigate the complexities of modern-day traffic environments effectively.

Remember, safe driving is a shared responsibility that impacts everyone. By embracing the principles outlined in this handbook, drivers can contribute to safer roads, reduce accidents, and ultimately, enhance the quality of life for themselves and others in their communities.

Drive safely, stay informed, and enjoy the journey ahead.

Made in the USA
Middletown, DE
06 September 2024

60495475R00096